LIKE MOST GREAT IDEAS, THIS ONE BEGAN WITH A

BEER

(ACTUALLY, IT WAS MORE LIKE 2,000)

When I first attended the world's largest beer festival, I was overwhelmed by the sheer quantity of craft beers on tap. There was no way I could taste (let alone remember) them all later. And I wasn't going to be that guy with the three-ring binder full of beer notes, either. So I came up with a pocket-size notebook that lets beer aficionados quickly record tasting notes so they can get back to tasting—and enjoying. Each of the notebooks in this pack has enough room to record your thoughts on 33 different beers. Try it, I think you'll like it.

D1537046

HOW TO USE

(AND GET A LOT MORE

STARE

The first step in evaluating a beer is often the most . . . ahem . . . overlooked. Use your eyes! How does the beer look?

Is it cloudy or clear, or is it completely opaque? What about the head, the froth at the top of the beer? Is it very fine, with small bubbles, like whipped cream? Or are the bubbles large, like pebbles? How thick is the head?

The answers to some of these questions will give you clues to the beer's flavors before you sip, and provide plenty of content for the "Appearance" areas in this book.

SNIFF

Farther down your face is a very helpful tool—your nose. Aroma is a huge part of the way humans experience flavor, and it, too, provides useful clues to better understanding your beer.

Take a few short sniffs of your beverage, getting up close and personal with the glass (you are using a glass, right?).

Be sure to choose the right type of glass for the beer you are consuming, as it is typically designed to deliver aromatics directly to your schnoz.

MY FAVORITE GLASS FOR TASTING IS A TULIP-STYLE
GLASS. AN ETCHED AREA ON THE BOTTOM PROVIDES
WHAT'S CALLED A "NUCLEATION SITE" THAT HELPS
RELEASE TRAPPED CARBONATION. THE GAS CARRIES
AROMA WITH IT AS IT MOVES UP THROUGH THE BEER.

THIS BOOK

FROM THE BEERS YOU TRY)

. . . .

SIP

Finally, it's time to have a drink. Take that first sip and swirl it around your mouth a bit. Some folks like to draw air through the beer while it's in their mouths, which sounds a bit like spitting inside out. Me, I like to lean back a bit and maybe even close my eyes to focus on the flavors I'm experiencing. Most really great beers (think Belgian), like really great stories, have a beginning, a middle, and an end (also called the aftertaste).

What other flavors does the beer remind you of? When people say a beer tastes like "leather" or "tobacco," it doesn't mean the beer actually contains those materials, but it does leave that kind of a sense memory with the consumer. The flavor wheel shown

on each spread in the journal provides a few common flavors and textures present to some degree in most beers. Be creative—there are no right or wrong answers and everyone's taste buds are unique!

MARK A DOT ON EACH SPOKE OF THE FLAVOR WHEEL INDICATING THE PRESENCE OR ABSENCE OF A FLAVOR (01 IS LOW FLAVOR). WHEN DONE, CONNECT THE DOTS! A BELGIAN DUBBEL IS SHOWN.

BEER NAME

BREWER

ORIGIN . . . .   **RATING** ☆☆☆☆☆

STATS
PRICE
IBU
ABV

SERVING VESSEL
☐ DRAFT
☐ CASK
☐ BOTTLE
☐ CAN
☐ GROWLER

FLAVOR WHEEL

ALCOHOLIC/
SOLVENT
LINGER · DARK FRUIT
BODY · CITRUS FRUIT
DRY · HOPPY
BITTER · FLORAL
SOUR · SPICY
SWEET · HERBAL
BURNT · MALTY
TOFFEE

0.5 0.4 0.3 0.2 0.1

CONSUMPTION VESSEL

SHAKER IMPERIAL TULIP PILSNER MUG   I WAS CAMPING   OTHER

APPEARANCE

....

....

....

....

AROMA

....

....

....

....

....

....

FLAVOR

....

....

....

....

....

BEER NAME ....

....

BREWER ....

ORIGIN .... **RATING** ☆☆☆☆☆

STATS
PRICE
IBU
ABV

FLAVOR WHEEL

SERVING VESSEL
☐ DRAFT
☐ CASK
☐ BOTTLE
☐ CAN
☐ GROWLER

CONSUMPTION VESSEL

SHAKER IMPERIAL TULIP PILSNER MUG   I WAS CAMPING   OTHER

APPEARANCE

....

....

....

....

AROMA

....

....

....

....

....

FLAVOR

....

....

....

....

SITUATION

SAMPLED

....

AT

....

WITH

COLOR METER

BLACK

WALNUT

MAHOGANY

CHERRY

CARAMEL

AMBER

GOLD

HONEY

STRAW

CLEAR

BEER NAME ....

....

BREWER ....

ORIGIN .... RATING ☆☆☆☆☆

STATS		FLAVOR WHEEL

STATS

PRICE

IBU

ABV

SERVING VESSEL

- [ ] DRAFT
- [ ] CASK
- [ ] BOTTLE
- [ ] CAN
- [ ] GROWLER

FLAVOR WHEEL

ALCOHOLIC/SOLVENT · DARK FRUIT · CITRUS FRUIT · HOPPY · FLORAL · SPICY · HERBAL · MALTY · TOFFEE · BURNT · SWEET · SOUR · BITTER · DRY · BODY · LINGER

CONSUMPTION VESSEL

SHAKER   IMPERIAL   TULIP   PILSNER   MUG   I WAS CAMPING   OTHER

APPEARANCE

. . . .

. . . .

. . . .

. . . .

AROMA

. . . .

. . . .

. . . .

. . . .

. . . .

FLAVOR

. . . .

. . . .

. . . .

. . . .

. . . .

SITUATION

SAMPLED

AT

WITH

COLOR METER

BLACK

WALNUT

MAHOGANY

CHERRY

CARAMEL

AMBER

GOLD

HONEY

STRAW

CLEAR

BEER NAME ....

....

BREWER ....

ORIGIN .... RATING ☆☆☆☆☆

STATS
PRICE
IBU
ABV

FLAVOR WHEEL

ALCOHOLIC/SOLVENT
LINGER
DARK FRUIT
BODY
CITRUS FRUIT
DRY
HOPPY
BITTER
FLORAL
SOUR
SPICY
SWEET
HERBAL
BURNT
MALTY
TOFFEE

SERVING VESSEL

☐ DRAFT
☐ CASK
☐ BOTTLE
☐ CAN
☐ GROWLER

CONSUMPTION VESSEL

SHAKER IMPERIAL TULIP PILSNER MUG I WAS CAMPING OTHER

APPEARANCE

. . . .

. . . .

. . . .

. . . .

AROMA

. . . .

. . . .

. . . .

. . . .

. . . .

FLAVOR

. . . .

. . . .

. . . .

. . . .

. . . .

SITUATION

SAMPLED

. . . .

AT

. . . .

WITH

COLOR METER

BLACK

WALNUT

MAHOGANY

CHERRY

CARAMEL

AMBER

GOLD

HONEY

STRAW

CLEAR

BEER NAME ....

....

BREWER ....

ORIGIN .... RATING ☆☆☆☆☆

STATS
PRICE
IBU
ABV

SERVING VESSEL

- ☐ DRAFT
- ☐ CASK
- ☐ BOTTLE
- ☐ CAN
- ☐ GROWLER

FLAVOR WHEEL

ALCOHOLIC/
SOLVENT
LINGER   DARK FRUIT
BODY   CITRUS
              FRUIT
DRY   HOPPY
BITTER   FLORAL
SOUR   SPICY
SWEET   HERBAL
BURNT   MALTY
     TOFFEE

CONSUMPTION VESSEL

SHAKER IMPERIAL TULIP PILSNER MUG   I WAS CAMPING   OTHER

APPEARANCE

. . . .

. . . .

. . . .

. . . .

AROMA

. . . .

. . . .

. . . .

. . . .

. . . .

FLAVOR

. . . .

. . . .

. . . .

. . . .

SITUATION

SAMPLED

. . . .

AT

. . . .

WITH

COLOR METER

- BLACK
- WALNUT
- MAHOGANY
- CHERRY
- CARAMEL
- AMBER
- GOLD
- HONEY
- STRAW
- CLEAR

BEER NAME ....

....

BREWER ....

ORIGIN .... **RATING** ☆☆☆☆☆

STATS	FLAVOR WHEEL
PRICE	
IBU	
ABV	

SERVING VESSEL

- ☐ DRAFT
- ☐ CASK
- ☐ BOTTLE
- ☐ CAN
- ☐ GROWLER

FLAVOR WHEEL

ALCOHOLIC/
SOLVENT
LINGER — DARK FRUIT
BODY — CITRUS FRUIT
DRY — HOPPY
BITTER — FLORAL
SOUR — SPICY
SWEET — HERBAL
BURNT — MALTY
TOFFEE

CONSUMPTION VESSEL

SHAKER   IMPERIAL   TULIP   PILSNER   MUG   I WAS CAMPING   OTHER

APPEARANCE

....
....
....
....

AROMA

....
....
....
....
....

FLAVOR

....
....
....
....
....

SITUATION

SAMPLED

....

AT

....

WITH

COLOR METER

- BLACK
- WALNUT
- MAHOGANY
- CHERRY
- CARAMEL
- AMBER
- GOLD
- HONEY
- STRAW
- CLEAR

BEER NAME . . . .

. . . .

BREWER . . . .

ORIGIN . . . . **RATING** ☆☆☆☆☆

STATS

PRICE
IBU
ABV

SERVING VESSEL

- ☐ DRAFT
- ☐ CASK
- ☐ BOTTLE
- ☐ CAN
- ☐ GROWLER

FLAVOR WHEEL

ALCOHOLIC/ SOLVENT
LINGER — DARK FRUIT
BODY — CITRUS FRUIT
DRY — HOPPY
BITTER — FLORAL
SOUR — SPICY
SWEET — HERBAL
BURNT — MALTY
TOFFEE

0 5
0 4
0 3
0 2

CONSUMPTION VESSEL

SHAKER   IMPERIAL   TULIP   PILSNER   MUG | I WAS CAMPING | OTHER

APPEARANCE

. . . .

. . . .

. . . .

. . . .

AROMA

. . . .

. . . .

. . . .

. . . .

FLAVOR

. . . .

. . . .

. . . .

. . . .

SITUATION

SAMPLED

AT

WITH

COLOR METER

BLACK

WALNUT

MAHOGANY

CHERRY

CARAMEL

AMBER

GOLD

HONEY

STRAW

CLEAR

BEER NAME ....

....

BREWER ....

ORIGIN .... **RATING** ☆☆☆☆☆

STATS	FLAVOR WHEEL
PRICE	
IBU	
ABV	

FLAVOR WHEEL

ALCOHOLIC/SOLVENT
LINGER — DARK FRUIT
BODY — CITRUS FRUIT
DRY — HOPPY
BITTER — FLORAL
SOUR — SPICY
SWEET — HERBAL
BURNT — MALTY
TOFFEE

SERVING VESSEL

☐ DRAFT
☐ CASK
☐ BOTTLE
☐ CAN
☐ GROWLER

CONSUMPTION VESSEL

SHAKER   IMPERIAL   TULIP   PILSNER   MUG   I WAS CAMPING   OTHER

APPEARANCE

....

....

....

....

AROMA

....

....

....

....

FLAVOR

....

....

....

....

SITUATION

SAMPLED

....

AT

....

WITH

COLOR METER

BLACK

WALNUT

MAHOGANY

CHERRY

CARAMEL

AMBER

GOLD

HONEY

STRAW

CLEAR

BEER NAME ....

....

BREWER ....

ORIGIN .... RATING ☆☆☆☆☆

STATS
PRICE
IBU
ABV

SERVING VESSEL

- ☐ DRAFT
- ☐ CASK
- ☐ BOTTLE
- ☐ CAN
- ☐ GROWLER

FLAVOR WHEEL

ALCOHOLIC/
SOLVENT
LINGER · DARK FRUIT
BODY · CITRUS FRUIT
DRY · HOPPY
BITTER · FLORAL
SOUR · SPICY
SWEET · HERBAL
BURNT · MALTY
TOFFEE

0.2 0.3 0.4 0.5

CONSUMPTION VESSEL

SHAKER   IMPERIAL   TULIP   PILSNER   MUG   I WAS CAMPING   OTHER

APPEARANCE

. . . .

. . . .

. . . .

. . . .

AROMA

. . . .

. . . .

. . . .

. . . .

. . . .

FLAVOR

. . . .

. . . .

. . . .

. . . .

. . . .

SITUATION

SAMPLED

. . . .

AT

. . . .

WITH

COLOR METER

BLACK

WALNUT

MAHOGANY

CHERRY

CARAMEL

AMBER

GOLD

HONEY

STRAW

CLEAR

BEER NAME ....

....

BREWER ....

ORIGIN .... RATING ☆☆☆☆☆

STATS	FLAVOR WHEEL
PRICE	
IBU	
ABV	

FLAVOR WHEEL

ALCOHOLIC/
SOLVENT

LINGER — DARK FRUIT
BODY — CITRUS FRUIT
DRY — HOPPY
BITTER — FLORAL
SOUR — SPICY
SWEET — HERBAL
BURNT — MALTY
TOFFEE

0.5 0.4 0.3 0.2

SERVING VESSEL

- ☐ DRAFT
- ☐ CASK
- ☐ BOTTLE
- ☐ CAN
- ☐ GROWLER

CONSUMPTION VESSEL

SHAKER   IMPERIAL   TULIP   PILSNER   MUG   I WAS CAMPING   OTHER

APPEARANCE

. . . .

. . . .

. . . .

. . . .

AROMA

. . . .

. . . .

. . . .

. . . .

. . . .

FLAVOR

. . . .

. . . .

. . . .

. . . .

SITUATION

SAMPLED

. . . .

AT

. . . .

WITH

COLOR METER

- BLACK
- WALNUT
- MAHOGANY
- CHERRY
- CARAMEL
- AMBER
- GOLD
- HONEY
- STRAW
- CLEAR

BEER NAME ....

....

BREWER ....

ORIGIN .... RATING ☆☆☆☆☆

STATS
PRICE
IBU
ABV

SERVING VESSEL

- ☐ DRAFT
- ☐ CASK
- ☐ BOTTLE
- ☐ CAN
- ☐ GROWLER

FLAVOR WHEEL

ALCOHOLIC/SOLVENT
LINGER   DARK FRUIT
BODY   CITRUS FRUIT
DRY   HOPPY
BITTER   FLORAL
SOUR   SPICY
SWEET   HERBAL
BURNT   MALTY
TOFFEE

CONSUMPTION VESSEL

SHAKER   IMPERIAL   TULIP   PILSNER   MUG   I WAS CAMPING   OTHER

APPEARANCE

....

....

....

....

AROMA

....

....

....

....

....

FLAVOR

....

....

....

....

SITUATION

SAMPLED

....

AT

....

WITH

COLOR METER

BLACK

WALNUT

MAHOGANY

CHERRY

CARAMEL

AMBER

GOLD

HONEY

STRAW

CLEAR

BEER NAME ....

....

BREWER ....

ORIGIN .... **RATING** ☆☆☆☆☆

STATS
PRICE
IBU
ABV

SERVING VESSEL

- ☐ DRAFT
- ☐ CASK
- ☐ BOTTLE
- ☐ CAN
- ☐ GROWLER

FLAVOR WHEEL

ALCOHOLIC/
SOLVENT
LINGER · DARK FRUIT
BODY · CITRUS FRUIT
DRY · HOPPY
BITTER · FLORAL
SOUR · SPICY
SWEET · HERBAL
BURNT · MALTY
TOFFEE

CONSUMPTION VESSEL

SHAKER   IMPERIAL   TULIP   PILSNER   MUG   I WAS CAMPING   OTHER

APPEARANCE

....

....

....

....

AROMA

....

....

....

....

....

....

FLAVOR

....

....

....

....

....

COLOR METER

- BLACK
- WALNUT
- MAHOGANY
- CHERRY
- CARAMEL
- AMBER
- GOLD
- HONEY
- STRAW
- CLEAR

BEER NAME . . . .

. . . .

BREWER . . . .

ORIGIN . . . . RATING ☆☆☆☆☆

STATS
PRICE
IBU
ABV

SERVING VESSEL

☐ DRAFT
☐ CASK
☐ BOTTLE
☐ CAN
☐ GROWLER

FLAVOR WHEEL

ALCOHOLIC/
SOLVENT
LINGER   DARK FRUIT
BODY   CITRUS
                    FRUIT
DRY   HOPPY
0 1 2 3 4 5
BITTER   FLORAL
SOUR   SPICY
SWEET   HERBAL
BURNT   MALTY
    TOFFEE

CONSUMPTION VESSEL

SHAKER IMPERIAL TULIP PILSNER MUG   I WAS CAMPING   OTHER

APPEARANCE

....
....
....
....

AROMA

....
....
....
....
....

FLAVOR

....
....
....
....

SITUATION

SAMPLED
....
AT
....
WITH

COLOR METER

BLACK

WALNUT

MAHOGANY

CHERRY

CARAMEL

AMBER

GOLD

HONEY

STRAW

CLEAR

BEER NAME ....

....

BREWER ....

ORIGIN .... RATING ☆☆☆☆☆

STATS
PRICE
IBU
ABV

FLAVOR WHEEL

ALCOHOLIC/
SOLVENT
LINGER — DARK FRUIT
BODY — CITRUS FRUIT
DRY — HOPPY
BITTER — FLORAL
SOUR — SPICY
SWEET — HERBAL
BURNT — MALTY
TOFFEE

0.5 0.4 0.3 0.2

SERVING VESSEL

- ☐ DRAFT
- ☐ CASK
- ☐ BOTTLE
- ☐ CAN
- ☐ GROWLER

CONSUMPTION VESSEL

SHAKER   IMPERIAL   TULIP   PILSNER   MUG   I WAS CAMPING   OTHER

APPEARANCE

. . . .

. . . .

. . . .

. . . .

AROMA

. . . .

. . . .

. . . .

. . . .

FLAVOR

. . . .

. . . .

. . . .

. . . .

. . . .

SITUATION

SAMPLED

AT

WITH

COLOR METER

BLACK

WALNUT

MAHOGANY

CHERRY

CARAMEL

AMBER

GOLD

HONEY

STRAW

CLEAR

BEER NAME ....

....

BREWER ....

ORIGIN .... **RATING** ☆☆☆☆☆

STATS		FLAVOR WHEEL

STATS
PRICE
IBU
ABV

FLAVOR WHEEL

ALCOHOLIC/
SOLVENT

LINGER — DARK FRUIT

BODY — CITRUS FRUIT

DRY — HOPPY

BITTER — FLORAL

SOUR — SPICY

SWEET — HERBAL

BURNT — MALTY

TOFFEE

SERVING VESSEL

- ☐ DRAFT
- ☐ CASK
- ☐ BOTTLE
- ☐ CAN
- ☐ GROWLER

CONSUMPTION VESSEL

SHAKER   IMPERIAL   TULIP   PILSNER   MUG | I WAS CAMPING | OTHER

BEER NO. **81** of **99**

APPEARANCE

. . . .

. . . .

. . . .

. . . .

AROMA

. . . .

. . . .

. . . .

. . . .

FLAVOR

. . . .

. . . .

. . . .

. . . .

SITUATION
SAMPLED
AT
WITH

COLOR METER

- BLACK
- WALNUT
- MAHOGANY
- CHERRY
- CARAMEL
- AMBER
- GOLD
- HONEY
- STRAW
- CLEAR

BEER NAME ....

....

BREWER ....

ORIGIN .... **RATING** ☆☆☆☆☆

STATS
PRICE
IBU
ABV

SERVING VESSEL

- ☐ DRAFT
- ☐ CASK
- ☐ BOTTLE
- ☐ CAN
- ☐ GROWLER

FLAVOR WHEEL

ALCOHOLIC/
SOLVENT
LINGER DARK FRUIT
BODY CITRUS FRUIT
DRY HOPPY
BITTER FLORAL
SOUR SPICY
SWEET HERBAL
BURNT MALTY
TOFFEE

CONSUMPTION VESSEL

SHAKER IMPERIAL TULIP PILSNER MUG I WAS CAMPING OTHER

APPEARANCE

. . . .

. . . .

. . . .

. . . .

AROMA

. . . .

. . . .

. . . .

. . . .

FLAVOR

. . . .

. . . .

. . . .

. . . .

SITUATION

SAMPLED

AT

WITH

COLOR METER

BLACK

WALNUT

MAHOGANY

CHERRY

CARAMEL

AMBER

GOLD

HONEY

STRAW

CLEAR

BEER NAME ....

....

BREWER ....

ORIGIN .... **RATING** ☆☆☆☆☆

STATS
PRICE
IBU
ABV

FLAVOR WHEEL

SERVING VESSEL
☐ DRAFT
☐ CASK
☐ BOTTLE
☐ CAN
☐ GROWLER

CONSUMPTION VESSEL

SHAKER   IMPERIAL   TULIP   PILSNER   MUG   I WAS CAMPING   OTHER

APPEARANCE

....

....

....

....

AROMA

....

....

....

....

....

FLAVOR

....

....

....

....

....

SITUATION
SAMPLED
AT
WITH

COLOR METER
BLACK
WALNUT
MAHOGANY
CHERRY
CARAMEL
AMBER
GOLD
HONEY
STRAW
CLEAR

BEER NAME ....

....

BREWER ....

ORIGIN .... RATING ☆☆☆☆☆

STATS
PRICE
IBU
ABV

FLAVOR WHEEL

ALCOHOLIC/
SOLVENT
LINGER   DARK FRUIT
BODY   CITRUS
                        FRUIT
DRY   HOPPY
BITTER   FLORAL
SOUR   SPICY
SWEET   HERBAL
BURNT   MALTY
TOFFEE

0.5 0.4 0.3 0.2 0.1

SERVING VESSEL
☐ DRAFT
☐ CASK
☐ BOTTLE
☐ CAN
☐ GROWLER

CONSUMPTION VESSEL

SHAKER   IMPERIAL   TULIP   PILSNER   MUG   I WAS CAMPING   OTHER

APPEARANCE

....
....
....
....

AROMA

....
....
....
....
....

FLAVOR

....
....
....
....
....
....

COLOR METER

BLACK

WALNUT

MAHOGANY

CHERRY

CARAMEL

AMBER

GOLD

HONEY

STRAW

CLEAR

BEER NAME ....

....

BREWER ....

ORIGIN .... RATING ☆☆☆☆☆

STATS
PRICE
IBU
ABV

SERVING VESSEL

- ☐ DRAFT
- ☐ CASK
- ☐ BOTTLE
- ☐ CAN
- ☐ GROWLER

FLAVOR WHEEL

ALCOHOLIC/SOLVENT
DARK FRUIT
LINGER
CITRUS FRUIT
BODY
HOPPY
DRY
FLORAL
BITTER
SPICY
SOUR
HERBAL
SWEET
MALTY
BURNT
TOFFEE

CONSUMPTION VESSEL

SHAKER   IMPERIAL   TULIP   PILSNER   MUG   I WAS CAMPING   OTHER

APPEARANCE

. . . .

. . . .

. . . .

. . . .

AROMA

. . . .

. . . .

. . . .

. . . .

. . . .

FLAVOR

. . . .

. . . .

. . . .

. . . .

. . . .

SITUATION

SAMPLED

. . . .

AT

. . . .

WITH

COLOR METER

BLACK

WALNUT

MAHOGANY

CHERRY

CARAMEL

AMBER

GOLD

HONEY

STRAW

CLEAR

BEER NAME ....

....

BREWER ....

ORIGIN .... RATING ☆☆☆☆☆

STATS	FLAVOR WHEEL
PRICE	
IBU	
ABV	

FLAVOR WHEEL

ALCOHOLIC/
SOLVENT
LINGER   DARK FRUIT
BODY   CITRUS
FRUIT
0 5
0 4
DRY   0 3   HOPPY
0 2
BITTER   FLORAL
SOUR   SPICY
SWEET   HERBAL
BURNT   MALTY
TOFFEE

SERVING VESSEL

☐ DRAFT
☐ CASK
☐ BOTTLE
☐ CAN
☐ GROWLER

CONSUMPTION VESSEL

SHAKER   IMPERIAL   TULIP   PILSNER   MUG   I WAS CAMPING   OTHER

APPEARANCE

....
....
....
....

AROMA

....
....
....
....
....

FLAVOR

....
....
....
....
....
....

SITUATION

SAMPLED
....
AT
....
WITH

COLOR METER

BLACK

WALNUT

MAHOGANY

CHERRY

CARAMEL

AMBER

GOLD

HONEY

STRAW

CLEAR

BEER NAME

...

BREWER ...

ORIGIN ...   RATING ☆☆☆☆☆

STATS
PRICE
IBU
ABV

FLAVOR WHEEL

ALCOHOLIC/SOLVENT
LINGER — DARK FRUIT
BODY — CITRUS FRUIT
DRY — HOPPY
BITTER — FLORAL
SOUR — SPICY
SWEET — HERBAL
BURNT — MALTY
TOFFEE

SERVING VESSEL

- [ ] DRAFT
- [ ] CASK
- [ ] BOTTLE
- [ ] CAN
- [ ] GROWLER

CONSUMPTION VESSEL

SHAKER   IMPERIAL   TULIP   PILSNER   MUG   I WAS CAMPING   OTHER

APPEARANCE

....
....
....
....

AROMA

....
....
....
....
....
....

FLAVOR

....
....
....
....
....

COLOR METER

BLACK

WALNUT

MAHOGANY

CHERRY

CARAMEL

AMBER

GOLD

HONEY

STRAW

CLEAR

BEER NAME ....

....

BREWER ....

ORIGIN .... RATING ☆☆☆☆☆

STATS
PRICE
IBU
ABV

FLAVOR WHEEL

ALCOHOLIC/SOLVENT
LINGER · DARK FRUIT
BODY · CITRUS FRUIT
DRY · HOPPY
BITTER · FLORAL
SOUR · SPICY
SWEET · HERBAL
BURNT · MALTY
TOFFEE

SERVING VESSEL

☐ DRAFT
☐ CASK
☐ BOTTLE
☐ CAN
☐ GROWLER

CONSUMPTION VESSEL

SHAKER   IMPERIAL   TULIP   PILSNER   MUG   I WAS CAMPING   OTHER

APPEARANCE

....
....
....
....

AROMA

....
....
....
....

FLAVOR

....
....
....
....
....

SITUATION

SAMPLED

....

AT

....

WITH

COLOR METER

BLACK

WALNUT

MAHOGANY

CHERRY

CARAMEL

AMBER

GOLD

HONEY

STRAW

CLEAR

BEER NAME ....

....

BREWER ....

ORIGIN .... RATING ☆☆☆☆☆

STATS	FLAVOR WHEEL
PRICE	
IBU	
ABV	

FLAVOR WHEEL

ALCOHOLIC/
SOLVENT
LINGER   DARK FRUIT
BODY   CITRUS
FRUIT
DRY   HOPPY
BITTER   FLORAL
SOUR   SPICY
SWEET   HERBAL
BURNT   MALTY
TOFFEE

SERVING VESSEL

☐ DRAFT
☐ CASK
☐ BOTTLE
☐ CAN
☐ GROWLER

CONSUMPTION VESSEL

SHAKER IMPERIAL TULIP PILSNER MUG   I WAS CAMPING   OTHER

APPEARANCE

....

....

....

....

AROMA

....

....

....

....

....

FLAVOR

....

....

....

....

....

SITUATION

SAMPLED

....

AT

....

WITH

COLOR METER

BLACK

WALNUT

MAHOGANY

CHERRY

CARAMEL

AMBER

GOLD

HONEY

STRAW

CLEAR

BEER NAME ....

....

BREWER ....

ORIGIN .... **RATING** ☆☆☆☆☆

STATS
PRICE
IBU
ABV

SERVING VESSEL

- [ ] DRAFT
- [ ] CASK
- [ ] BOTTLE
- [ ] CAN
- [ ] GROWLER

FLAVOR WHEEL

ALCOHOLIC/
SOLVENT
LINGER · DARK FRUIT
BODY · CITRUS FRUIT
DRY · HOPPY
BITTER · FLORAL
SOUR · SPICY
SWEET · HERBAL
BURNT · MALTY
TOFFEE

CONSUMPTION VESSEL

SHAKER   IMPERIAL   TULIP   PILSNER   MUG | I WAS CAMPING | OTHER

APPEARANCE

....

....

....

....

AROMA

....

....

....

....

....

FLAVOR

....

....

....

....

....

COLOR METER

- BLACK
- WALNUT
- MAHOGANY
- CHERRY
- CARAMEL
- AMBER
- GOLD
- HONEY
- STRAW
- CLEAR

BEER NAME ....

....

BREWER ....

ORIGIN .... RATING ☆☆☆☆☆

STATS
PRICE
IBU
ABV

FLAVOR WHEEL

ALCOHOLIC/
SOLVENT
LINGER   DARK FRUIT
BODY   CITRUS
FRUIT
DRY   HOPPY
BITTER   FLORAL
SOUR   SPICY
SWEET   HERBAL
BURNT   MALTY
TOFFEE

SERVING VESSEL

- ☐ DRAFT
- ☐ CASK
- ☐ BOTTLE
- ☐ CAN
- ☐ GROWLER

CONSUMPTION VESSEL

SHAKER   IMPERIAL   TULIP   PILSNER   MUG   I WAS CAMPING   OTHER

APPEARANCE

. . . .

. . . .

. . . .

. . . .

AROMA

. . . .

. . . .

. . . .

. . . .

. . . .

FLAVOR

. . . .

. . . .

. . . .

. . . .

. . . .

SITUATION

SAMPLED

AT

WITH

COLOR METER

BLACK

WALNUT

MAHOGANY

CHERRY

CARAMEL

AMBER

GOLD

HONEY

STRAW

CLEAR

BEER NAME ....

....

BREWER ....

ORIGIN .... **RATING** ☆☆☆☆☆

STATS	FLAVOR WHEEL

STATS
PRICE
IBU
ABV

SERVING VESSEL

- ☐ DRAFT
- ☐ CASK
- ☐ BOTTLE
- ☐ CAN
- ☐ GROWLER

FLAVOR WHEEL

ALCOHOLIC/
SOLVENT
LINGER · DARK FRUIT
BODY · CITRUS FRUIT
· HOPPY
DRY ·
BITTER · · FLORAL
SOUR · · SPICY
SWEET · · HERBAL
BURNT · MALTY
TOFFEE

0 5 / 0 4 / 0 3 / 0 2 / 0 1

CONSUMPTION VESSEL

SHAKER IMPERIAL TULIP PILSNER MUG | I WAS CAMPING | OTHER

APPEARANCE

. . . .

. . . .

. . . .

. . . .

AROMA

. . . .

. . . .

. . . .

. . . .

FLAVOR

. . . .

. . . .

. . . .

. . . .

SITUATION

SAMPLED

AT

WITH

COLOR METER

BLACK

WALNUT

MAHOGANY

CHERRY

CARAMEL

AMBER

GOLD

HONEY

STRAW

CLEAR

BEER NAME ....

....

BREWER ....

ORIGIN .... **RATING** ☆☆☆☆☆

STATS
PRICE
IBU
ABV

SERVING VESSEL

☐ DRAFT
☐ CASK
☐ BOTTLE
☐ CAN
☐ GROWLER

FLAVOR WHEEL

ALCOHOLIC/
SOLVENT
LINGER   DARK FRUIT
BODY   CITRUS
                        FRUIT
DRY   HOPPY
BITTER   FLORAL
SOUR   SPICY
SWEET   HERBAL
BURNT   MALTY
        TOFFEE

0.5 0.4 0.3 0.2

CONSUMPTION VESSEL

SHAKER IMPERIAL TULIP PILSNER MUG   I WAS CAMPING   OTHER

APPEARANCE

....
....
....
....

AROMA

....
....
....
....
....

FLAVOR

....
....
....
....
....

SITUATION

SAMPLED
....
AT
....
WITH

COLOR METER

BLACK

WALNUT

MAHOGANY

CHERRY

CARAMEL

AMBER

GOLD

HONEY

STRAW

CLEAR

BEER NAME ....

....

BREWER ....

ORIGIN .... **RATING** ☆☆☆☆☆

STATS	FLAVOR WHEEL
PRICE	
IBU	
ABV	

STATS

PRICE

IBU

ABV

SERVING VESSEL

- ☐ DRAFT
- ☐ CASK
- ☐ BOTTLE
- ☐ CAN
- ☐ GROWLER

FLAVOR WHEEL

ALCOHOLIC/
SOLVENT

LINGER · DARK FRUIT
BODY · CITRUS FRUIT
DRY · HOPPY
BITTER · FLORAL
SOUR · SPICY
SWEET · HERBAL
BURNT · MALTY
TOFFEE

0.5 0.4 0.3 0.2

CONSUMPTION VESSEL

SHAKER   IMPERIAL   TULIP   PILSNER   MUG   I WAS CAMPING   OTHER

APPEARANCE

....
....
....
....

AROMA

....
....
....
....
....

FLAVOR

....
....
....
....
....

COLOR METER

BLACK

WALNUT

MAHOGANY

CHERRY

CARAMEL

AMBER

GOLD

HONEY

STRAW

CLEAR

BEER NAME ....

....

BREWER ....

ORIGIN .... **RATING** ☆☆☆☆☆

STATS
PRICE
IBU
ABV

SERVING VESSEL

- ☐ DRAFT
- ☐ CASK
- ☐ BOTTLE
- ☐ CAN
- ☐ GROWLER

FLAVOR WHEEL

ALCOHOLIC/
SOLVENT
LINGER — DARK FRUIT
BODY — CITRUS FRUIT
— HOPPY
DRY — FLORAL
BITTER —
SOUR — SPICY
SWEET — HERBAL
BURNT — MALTY
TOFFEE

0.5 0.4 0.3 0.2

CONSUMPTION VESSEL

SHAKER   IMPERIAL   TULIP   PILSNER   MUG   I WAS CAMPING   OTHER

APPEARANCE

....
....
....
....

AROMA

....
....
....
....
....
....

FLAVOR

....
....
....
....
....
....
....

COLOR METER

BLACK
WALNUT
MAHOGANY
CHERRY
CARAMEL
AMBER
GOLD
HONEY
STRAW
CLEAR

BEER NAME ....

....

BREWER ....

ORIGIN .... **RATING** ☆☆☆☆☆

STATS	FLAVOR WHEEL
PRICE	
IBU	
ABV	

STATS

| PRICE |
| IBU |
| ABV |

SERVING VESSEL

- ☐ DRAFT
- ☐ CASK
- ☐ BOTTLE
- ☐ CAN
- ☐ GROWLER

FLAVOR WHEEL

ALCOHOLIC/
SOLVENT
LINGER — DARK FRUIT
BODY
CITRUS
FRUIT
HOPPY
DRY
BITTER — FLORAL
SOUR
SPICY
SWEET
HERBAL
BURNT — MALTY
TOFFEE

0.5 0.4 0.3 0.2

CONSUMPTION VESSEL

SHAKER IMPERIAL TULIP PILSNER MUG   I WAS CAMPING   OTHER

APPEARANCE

. . . .

. . . .

. . . .

. . . .

AROMA

. . . .

. . . .

. . . .

. . . .

. . . .

FLAVOR

. . . .

. . . .

. . . .

. . . .

. . . .

SITUATION

SAMPLED

. . . .

AT

. . . .

WITH

COLOR METER

BLACK

WALNUT

MAHOGANY

CHERRY

CARAMEL

AMBER

GOLD

HONEY

STRAW

CLEAR

BEER NAME ....

....

BREWER ....

ORIGIN .... **RATING** ☆☆☆☆☆

STATS
PRICE
IBU
ABV

SERVING VESSEL

- [ ] DRAFT
- [ ] CASK
- [ ] BOTTLE
- [ ] CAN
- [ ] GROWLER

FLAVOR WHEEL

ALCOHOLIC/
SOLVENT
LINGER — DARK FRUIT
BODY — CITRUS FRUIT
DRY — HOPPY
BITTER — FLORAL
SOUR — SPICY
SWEET — HERBAL
BURNT — MALTY
TOFFEE

0.5
0.4
0.3
0.2

CONSUMPTION VESSEL

SHAKER   IMPERIAL   TULIP   PILSNER   MUG   I WAS CAMPING   OTHER

APPEARANCE

....

....

....

....

AROMA

....

....

....

....

....

FLAVOR

....

....

....

....

COLOR METER

BLACK

WALNUT

MAHOGANY

CHERRY

CARAMEL

AMBER

GOLD

HONEY

STRAW

CLEAR

BEER NAME ....

....

BREWER ....

ORIGIN .... **RATING** ☆☆☆☆☆

STATS
PRICE
IBU
ABV

SERVING VESSEL

- ☐ DRAFT
- ☐ CASK
- ☐ BOTTLE
- ☐ CAN
- ☐ GROWLER

FLAVOR WHEEL

ALCOHOLIC/SOLVENT — DARK FRUIT — CITRUS FRUIT — HOPPY — FLORAL — SPICY — HERBAL — MALTY — TOFFEE — BURNT — SWEET — SOUR — BITTER — DRY — BODY — LINGER

CONSUMPTION VESSEL

SHAKER IMPERIAL TULIP PILSNER MUG I WAS CAMPING OTHER

APPEARANCE

....

....

....

....

AROMA

....

....

....

....

....

....

FLAVOR

....

....

....

....

....

....

....

SITUATION

SAMPLED

AT

WITH

COLOR METER

BLACK

WALNUT

MAHOGANY

CHERRY

CARAMEL

AMBER

GOLD

HONEY

STRAW

CLEAR

BEER NAME ....

....

BREWER ....

ORIGIN .... RATING ☆☆☆☆☆

STATS
PRICE
IBU
ABV

SERVING VESSEL

- ☐ DRAFT
- ☐ CASK
- ☐ BOTTLE
- ☐ CAN
- ☐ GROWLER

FLAVOR WHEEL

ALCOHOLIC/SOLVENT
LINGER · DARK FRUIT
BODY · CITRUS FRUIT
DRY · HOPPY
BITTER · FLORAL
SOUR · SPICY
SWEET · HERBAL
BURNT · MALTY
TOFFEE

CONSUMPTION VESSEL

SHAKER   IMPERIAL   TULIP   PILSNER   MUG   I WAS CAMPING   OTHER

APPEARANCE

. . . .

. . . .

. . . .

. . . .

AROMA

. . . .

. . . .

. . . .

. . . .

FLAVOR

. . . .

. . . .

. . . .

. . . .

SITUATION

SAMPLED

AT

WITH

COLOR METER

BLACK

WALNUT

MAHOGANY

CHERRY

CARAMEL

AMBER

GOLD

HONEY

STRAW

CLEAR

AROUND THE WORLD

BEERS BY CONTINENT

- ☐ AFRICA
- ☐ ANTARCTICA
- ☐ ASIA
- ☐ AUSTRALIA
- ☐ EUROPE
- ☐ NORTH AMERICA
- ☐ SOUTH AMERICA

IN 33 BEERS

As you move through this journal, you'll surely be stretching your taste buds across beer styles, but, thanks to the resurgence of beer culture around the world, you'll be crossing international boundaries, too. Use this map to mark the beers you try based on where they're brewed. Bonus points for finding a beer brewed on the most southerly continent . . . rumor has it that the researchers at McMurdo Station in Antarctica have been known to home-brew on occasion.

THE END ... OR IS IT?

Whew! Another 33 Beers down! You deserve ... another beer!

Write down your favorite beers (and your least favorite) from this book for quick reference the next time you're at the beer store. That way, you'll be drinking more good beer and less ... Liller Mite.

FAVORITE BEERS	
1	☆☆☆☆☆
2	☆☆☆☆☆
3	☆☆☆☆☆
4	☆☆☆☆☆
5	☆☆☆☆☆

LEAST FAVORITE BEERS	
29	☆☆☆☆☆
30	☆☆☆☆☆
31	☆☆☆☆☆
32	☆☆☆☆☆
33	☆☆☆☆☆